BOSTON CELTICS

AARON FRISCH

Published by Creative Education
P.O. Box 227
Mankato, Minnesota 56002
Creative Education is an imprint of The Creative Company.

DESIGN AND PRODUCTION BY ZENO DESIGN

PHOTOGRAPHS BY Corbis (Bettmann), Getty Images (NBAE)

LIBRARY OF CONGRESS CATALOGING-IN-PUBLICATION DATA

Frisch, Aaron.
Boston Celtics / by Aaron Frisch.
p. cm. — (NBA champions)
Includes index.
ISBN-13: 978-1-58341-504-7
1. Boston Celtics (Basketball team)—History.
2. Basketball—History. I. Title.

GV885.52.B67F75 2007
796.323'640974461—dc22   2006020235

First edition

9 8 7 6 5 4 3 2 1

COVER PHOTO: *Forward Paul Pierce*

NBA

4

THE CELTICS are a professional basketball team in the National Basketball Association (NBA). They play in Boston, Massachusetts. Boston is next to the ocean. It is one of the oldest cities in the United States.

The city of Boston is almost 400 years old ▷

BOSTON CELTICS

THE CELTICS' arena is called TD Banknorth Garden. Their uniforms are green and white. The Celtics play lots of games against teams called the 76ers, Knicks, Nets, and Raptors.

◁ The Celtics' old arena was called Boston Garden

7

THE CELTICS played their first season in 1946. They soon got a clever coach named Red Auerbach *[AR-bok]*. They also got a point guard named Bob Cousy *[KOO-zee]*. Cousy was fast and could throw tricky passes.

Bob Cousy was a good team leader on the court ▷

9

THE CELTICS became a powerful team when they added center Bill Russell. He won an award as the NBA's best player five times. In 1957, he helped the Celtics win their first NBA championship.

11

◁ Bill Russell was quick and blocked lots of shots

THE CELTICS were the best team in the NBA in the 1960s. They won the NBA championship 9 times in 10 seasons! The Celtics played many famous games against the Los Angeles Lakers. The Celtics and Lakers became great rivals.

The Celtics and Lakers are two of the best teams ever ▷

NBA CHAMPIONS   1957   1959–1966   1968   1969   1974   1976   1981   1984   1986

AFTER Russell retired, Boston got some new players. John Havlicek [HAV-lih-chek] was a forward who scored a lot and played tight defense. He helped the Celtics win the NBA championship in 1974 and 1976.

◁ John Havlicek played for the Celtics for 16 years

15

16

THE CELTICS' next star player was Larry Bird. He was one of the best shooters ever. He was one of the most popular NBA players, too. Bird helped the Celtics win three more NBA championships in the 1980s.

Larry Bird made lots of long, three-point shots ▷

NBA CHAMPIONS 1957 1959 1966 1968 1969 1974 1976 1981 1984 1986

17

18

THE CELTICS were not as good after that. They had some exciting players, such as forward Reggie Lewis. But they could not win the championship again.

◁ **Reggie Lewis was one of the NBA's fastest players**

20

PAUL PIERCE was another good Celtics player. He was a forward who usually scored more than 20 points a game. The Celtics have many new players today. Boston fans hope that their team will win the NBA championship again soon!

Paul Pierce could score in lots of ways ▷

GLOSSARY

ARENA   a building with lots of seats where teams play basketball

NATIONAL BASKETBALL ASSOCIATION (NBA)
a group of basketball teams that play against each other; there are 30
teams in the NBA today

PROFESSIONAL   a person or team that gets paid to play or work

RETIRED   stopped playing for good

RIVALS   teams that play extra hard against each other

FUN FACTS

TEAM COLORS: Green and white

HOME ARENA: TD Banknorth Garden

CONFERENCE/DIVISION: Eastern Conference, Atlantic Division

FIRST SEASON: 1946

NBA CHAMPIONSHIPS: 1957, 1959, 1960, 1961, 1962, 1963, 1964, 1965, 1966, 1968, 1969, 1974, 1976, 1981, 1984, 1986

GREAT PLAYERS: Bill Russell (center), John Havlicek (forward), Larry Bird (forward)

NBA WEB SITE FOR KIDS: http://www.nba.com/kids/

TEAM NAME: The Celtics got their name because lots of people from Ireland lived in Boston. "Celtics" is a word that describes people from Ireland.

NBA CHAMPIONS · 1957 1959–1966 1968 1969 1974 1976 1981 1984 1986

23

INDEX